For Marjie Podzielinski, Librarian Goddess
—K. K.

For my mom, who led with her voice
and my dad who led by example
—A. B.

A
atheneum

ATHENEUM BOOKS FOR YOUNG READERS
An imprint of Simon & Schuster Children's Publishing Division
1230 Avenue of the Americas, New York, New York 10020
Text copyright © 2020 by Kathleen Krull
Illustrations copyright © 2020 by Alexandra Bye
All rights reserved, including the right of reproduction in whole or in part in any form.
ATHENEUM BOOKS FOR YOUNG READERS is a trademark of Simon & Schuster, Inc.
Atheneum logo is a trademark of Simon & Schuster, Inc.
For information about special discounts for bulk purchases, please contact
Simon & Schuster Special Sales at 1-866-506-1949 or business@simonandschuster.com.
The Simon & Schuster Speakers Bureau can bring authors to your live event. For more information or to book an event,
contact the Simon & Schuster Speakers Bureau at 1-866-248-3049 or visit our website at www.simonspeakers.com.
Book design by Chloë Foglia
The text for this book was set in Garamond.
The illustrations for this book were rendered digitally.
Manufactured in China
1121 SCP
4 6 8 10 9 7 5
Library of Congress Cataloging-in-Publication Data
Names: Krull, Kathleen, author. | Bye, Alexandra, illustrator.
Title: The only woman in the photo : Frances Perkins and her New Deal for America / Kathleen Krull ; illustrated by Alexandra Bye.
Other titles: Frances Perkins and her New Deal for America
Description: First edition. | New York : Simon & Schuster Books for Young Readers, [2019] | Audience: Ages 4–8.
Identifiers: LCCN 2018045302 (print) | LCCN 2018057091 (eBook) | ISBN 9781481491525 (eBook) | ISBN 9781481491518 (hardcover)
Subjects: LCSH: Perkins, Frances, 1880–1965. | United States. Department of Labor—Officials and employees—Biography—Juvenile
literature. | Women cabinet officers—United States—Biography—Juvenile literature. | Women social reformers—United States—Biography—
Juvenile literature. | New Deal, 1933–1939—Juvenile literature | Cabinet officers—United States—Biography—Juvenile literature. |
Social reformers—United States—Biography—Juvenile literature.
Classification: LCC HD8073.P38 (eBook) | LCC HD8073.P38 K78 2019 (print) | DDC 331.092 [B]—dc23
LC record available at https://lccn.loc.gov/2018045302

The Only WOMAN in the PHOTO

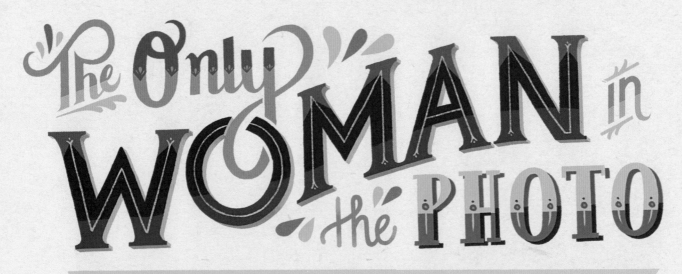

FRANCES PERKINS & HER NEW DEAL for AMERICA

Kathleen Krull

Alexandra Bye

 Atheneum Books for Young Readers

NEW YORK LONDON TORONTO SYDNEY NEW DELHI

Little Frances Perkins was shy. She couldn't speak up even when asking for a book at the library or a spool of thread at the store in her cozy New England town.

She was most comfortable around her grandmother, who encouraged her to always keep trying. She would say . . .

TAKE the HIGH GROUND IF SOMEONE INSULTS YOU & WHEN SOMEONE OPENS a DOOR TO YOU GO FORWARD

So, shy Frances tried her hardest in everything she did.

Frances was quiet, but she was a watcher and a listener.

She was sad to see young Irish immigrants being screamed at and chased by those who hated newcomers. She felt sorry that her best friend's family was not as well-off as hers. Her parents said that if you were poor it was your own fault. But Frances wondered.

She couldn't stand the thought of children going hungry or being in pain, and she couldn't see how it was their fault. She knew first aid, and other kids turned to her when they were hurt. She followed her grandmother's advice and always tried to help.

Frances was a thinker at a time when higher education for women was new. People feared that women's "delicate bodies" would suffer if their brains got too big.

But her father saw how smart Frances was. He taught her to read at an early age and encouraged her to go on learning.

In high school, she mastered tough classes, including Latin and Greek. She blossomed—from a whisperer to a star debater. The point was always to challenge herself.

Going to college meant the world to Frances, and a history course there shaped her future. The professor required students to observe the depressing conditions in the nearby paper and textile mills. Frances was horrified, especially at the small children toiling alongside adults.

The experience opened her eyes to other injustices in America, like those she'd glimpsed as a child. But "these were the days when nobody expected the government to do anything," she said.

Frances ached to help. To do that, she realized she had to make her voice heard, even when speaking made her uncomfortable. In speaking up, Frances was learning to lead.

Against her parents' wishes—they preferred she start husband-hunting—she moved to New York City and began working. A new way to help fight injustice, called social work, was flourishing there.

The more she saw, the more she wanted to help.

I had to do **SOMETHING** about the **UNNECESSARY** hazards to life,

UNNECESSARY POVERTY.

It was sort of **UP TO ME.**

She started off delivering milk and food to starving children, getting landlords to give a break to those unable to pay their rent, and asking for donations. In dangerous neighborhoods, she defended herself with the tip of her umbrella.

For these social justice issues to get proper attention, Frances believed women had to get more power. So she went even further. She was a fierce fighter for women's right to vote. She spoke out about suffrage on street corners, bringing her own grocery crate to stand on. She honed her speaking skills, projected her voice, and used humor to deflect hecklers.

After getting more education in social work and publishing her own articles on the subject, Frances kept working to protect others by taking a job gathering information on unsafe workplaces.

She visited more than a hundred bakeries, taking notes. Bread, donuts, and pies were baked in airless rooms with dirt floors.

Rats nibbled on bags of flour, and cats had kittens on the counters. Dirty water, instead of chocolate, dripped onto pastries. Frances saw sick workers bending over the dough and coughing. Children huddled there with their parents because they had nowhere else to go.

She wrote it all down in her report. When she presented it to New York's Board of Health, bakeries were forced to improve conditions.

But Frances didn't stop there. Next on her list was fire safety. She inspected twenty-six laundries, finding danger everywhere. This problem was urgent.

It became even more urgent after one horrible day in 1911. Thirty-year-old Frances was having tea with friends when the group heard the clanging of fire-truck bells and an unearthly shrieking.

She lifted up her long skirt and ran toward the scene of a fire. The Triangle Shirtwaist Factory was burning, and the management, worried about theft, had locked all the doors! The factory employed Italian and Jewish immigrants, mostly women and girls in their teens and early twenties, and they were all trapped.

The fire claimed a total of 146 victims. The youngest were only fourteen years old.

Frances was sick to her stomach—and then outraged. To her this was murder, a tragedy that could have been prevented. If no one else would become the voice for these women, Frances would try.

Witnessing the Triangle Shirtwaist Factory fire turned Frances Perkins into an activist, so intent on helping others that she was ready to enter the all-male world of politics.

Former president Theodore Roosevelt was heading up a committee on New York City workplace safety. He'd heard good things about Frances as an expert investigator, so he recommended her to run the committee. She began taking the others on tours of work sites to view firsthand the dangers of greedy managers not protecting their workers.

She studied the men she worked with, looking for ways to overcome prejudice. Some men would never treat her as an equal, but if she reminded them of their mothers, in her staid three-cornered hat, she seemed to have more success.

Her intense study of how men acted was worth it. The committee agreed with her, and the modern fire precautions we have today—glass cases with fire extinguishers, fire exits, fire drills, and water sprinklers—began to be required. The city passed the most comprehensive workplace-safety laws in the nation.

It wasn't long before Al Smith, the governor of New York State, rewarded Frances's hard work with her first big break in government. He appointed her to the commission that regulated workplaces across the whole state. She was "tongue-tied for a moment," but she decided to accept. The job was not just a grand opportunity to make her voice heard on the issues that mattered to her, but it was so significant that it made her the highest-paid woman to hold public office in the United States at the time!

In her new role, Frances kept arguing for change, helping to pass dozens of laws that made New York safer for workers in copper mines, construction sites, and factories all across the state.

In 1929, New York's new governor Franklin D. Roosevelt appointed Frances the state's industrial commissioner, overseeing more than 1,700 employees in seven cities.

And soon, it turned out, FDR would need Frances more than ever. When the stock market crashed on Black Tuesday, October 29, 1929, it propelled the nation into the Great Depression.

The country suffered as it never had before. About a third of working Americans lost their jobs, then many lost their homes. Frances visited encampments of miserable families living in cardboard boxes and tents.

President Herbert Hoover kept making reassuring statements, predicting that recovery was around the corner. Frances was furious—she knew it was not, and she had to speak up or else people would start blaming themselves for being out of work. In 1930, she called a press conference to announce that Hoover was wrong, and that she had the facts and numbers to prove it.

Yes, Frances Perkins had just challenged the president. Telegrams and phone calls poured in to criticize her, but she said,

I felt the SATISFACTION of someone who told the TRUTH

In the 1932 election, Hoover was defeated in a landslide by none other than Frances's boss: FDR.

And he wanted Frances as the secretary of labor in his cabinet of advisors. He was proposing a New Deal—a fresh start for Americans in need—and she was a crucial part of the plan.

At fifty-two years old, Frances hesitated. The challenge seemed extreme. And as the first woman ever to join a presidential cabinet, she would face a storm of criticism.

But her grandmother's advice sailed into her mind, and she knew what she had to do.

"The door might not be opened to a WOMAN again for a long, long time. And I had a kind of a DUTY to walk in & sit down in the chair that was offered."

Challenging herself and using her voice, she realized, would allow her to protect people across the nation, and inspire women at the same time.

So Frances decided she'd accept the job—if FDR allowed her to do it her way. She had been thinking up ideas for years. Now she wrote all her requests on slips of paper, a to-do list for helping the most vulnerable.

At their meeting, she held them up, and she watched the president's eyes to make sure he understood what she was planning. The scope of her list was breathtaking. It was nothing less than a restructuring of American society.

Their talk lasted one hour—until he finally said, "I'll back you."

Newspapers had headlines like

Sure enough, Frances was now one of the ten most powerful people in government in the whole country. Her Department of Labor was in charge of all matters concerning American workers.

On her first day on the job, she took control of her desk, only to find the drawers crawling with the largest cockroaches she had ever seen. It seemed a sign of how corrupt and inefficient the department had been.

She rolled up her sleeves, scrubbed out her desk, and plunged into working—basically around the clock.

At her first cabinet meeting, nervous about how best to make herself heard, Frances decided on a quiet approach: "I wanted to give the impression of being a quiet, orderly woman who didn't buzz-buzz all the time." As she had on her very first committee, she knew she would have to make the other men take her seriously.

Finally FDR turned to her with a smile. "Well, Miss Perkins, have you anything to say, anything to contribute?"

She spoke briefly about her recommendations for reducing unemployment, and after that the men treated her as an equal—sort of.

Some men in her department did threaten to resign rather than report to a woman. Others acted like schoolboys and passed silly notes about her during meetings.

One day, she testified before Congress, and a congressman remarked, "She's an awful smart woman, but I'd hate to be married to her."

When Frances heard about the insult, she laughed it off, retorting that "I hadn't asked him." She had a job to do.

The first hundred days were critical. Frances had two phones on her desk and would sometimes answer both at the same time. Mostly, though, she was out of her office, initiating a blizzard of big moves, an alphabet soup of agencies. The Civilian Conservation Corps, for example, put more than two million young people to work taking care of national resources: stocking rivers with fish, planting trees, and digging canals for flood control. With this and her many other undertakings, it was thrilling for her to see how directly she was helping people.

Wherever she was—at steel factories, on the docks with shipyard workers in California, testifying before Congress—she was a voice for calm. Her goal was to establish a sense of security during a nerve-racking crisis. She accepted every invitation to speak, feeling responsible for explaining the New Deal to the public.

She met with FDR every ten days or so. He liked to hear her advice in the form of a story—who specifically was going to be helped, what exactly would be the result of the action she recommended. With a story he could then relay to others, he would always support her latest idea.

Change was really happening.

Magazine headlines hailed "Fearless Frances." One called her "The Woman Nobody Knows"—giving her full credit for the New Deal.
In official pictures, she was usually the only woman in the photo.

SUNDAY *Leader*

WHO IS FRANCES PERKINS?

ONE DOLLAR

TIMES

FEARLESS FRANCES

NOVEMBER

Her most far-reaching dream became a reality in 1935 when FDR signed the life-changing Social Security Act into law. It established insurance for old age and for people who lost their jobs. It ensured compensation for those injured on the job. It guaranteed aid to the needy and disabled, and even children under eighteen in single-parent families. It was, she said, "a security structure which aims to protect our people against the major hazards of life."

It was basically her entire to-do list. She saw it as "a turning point in our national life—a turn from careless neglect of human values" toward people working together for the common good.

Hurdling one obstacle after another, boldly speaking up, she transformed the government into a force that helped protect people. On a gigantic scale, she had reached her childhood goal of helping others.

she declared, hoping to return to a quieter life. But FDR valued her too much to accept her resignation.

She was at his side from his first day as president to his last day, in 1945. In one of their final meetings, he was crying as he grasped her hand: "Frances, you have done awfully well. I know what you have been through. I know what you have accomplished. Thank you."

After his death, she was finally allowed to resign. She kept working for her causes and lecturing at universities, but out of the public eye.

"I haven't a flair for publicity," Frances said. She absolutely refused to write a book about herself. Once she said that seeing her picture in the newspaper "nearly kills me." She actually stomped on the camera of one photographer who took her picture despite her pleas not to.

So when Frances died after suffering a stroke in 1965, at age eighty-five, not many people remembered who she was and what she had accomplished.

Social Security, fire safety, workplace regulations, and many of the other laws that keep us safe are things we take for granted. But we should never forget the person who made them happen—a shy little girl who cared about others and grew up to protect them.

THE POWER of FRANCES PERKINS

Strand by strand, Frances Perkins (1880–1965) helped weave a safety net that protects all Americans to this day.

The odds against accomplishing what she did during her era are so high that we have to ask: How in the world did she do it? How did she come to be the only woman in the photo?

One factor that helped was a certain amount of luck—being in the right place at the right time. She was able to develop leadership skills at an all-women college at a time when the barriers to higher education for women were just starting to be dropped. The field of social work—a practical way of helping others and fighting for social justice—was also brand-new, fostered by women, and an ideal direction for her goals.

Perkins always insisted that she was a product of women who had influenced her, starting with her beloved grandmother. Mary Lyon (1797–1849), the founder of her college, Mount Holyoke, had as her motto: "Go forward, attempt great things, accomplish great things." Perkins drew inspiration from other women who came before her, such as Ida Tarbell (1857–1944), pioneer of investigative journalism, and Jane Addams (1860–1935), founder of the American profession of social work. But her biggest mentor and cheerleader, by far, was Florence Kelley (1859–1932), a pioneering social and political reformer. One of Kelley's speeches, said Perkins, "first opened my mind to the necessity for and the possibility of the work which became my vocation."

Perkins was also aided by the fact that, thanks to her hard work and glowing reputation, she had earned the support of a powerful man, a president so popular he was elected to four terms in office. For a man of his day, FDR was unusually open-minded toward women, perhaps due to being the son of a strong woman and husband to one of the most revered women in American history, Eleanor Roosevelt.

Additionally, she was working toward her goals during a time of severe crisis. The Depression made so many people so desperately poor that it effected a change in the country's ideas about being poor. Poverty wasn't a character flaw, after all. For the first time, many in government saw the need to help.

The time was right, but knowing the odds were against her as a woman, Frances also had to cultivate a certain amount of denial about it: "Being a woman has only bothered me in climbing trees." As much as possible, she just tried to ignore her gender and focus on her work. She found it helpful to fill a red envelope she called "The Male Mind" with notes about how men thought and how she could best make them listen.

Her work ethic was amazing, as was her lack of fear: "You just can't be afraid . . . if you're going to accomplish anything." Perkins also had the motivation of being the sole support of her husband and her daughter, both of whom had significant health problems.

Perhaps, above all, it was her voice and the striking way she was able to use it that led to her success. Speaking was her superpower—speaking up for herself, and then for others.

Frances was a powerful woman, so ahead of her time that many didn't know what to make of her. Combined, these elements helped her reach the goals she'd been working for her whole life. It would be another twenty years before another woman joined the president's cabinet.

Today the Department of Labor is housed in a building named for her, where a plaque reads: THIS BUILDING IS DEDICATED TO THE MEMORY OF FRANCES PERKINS, SECRETARY OF LABOR, 1933–1945, WHOSE LEGACY OF SOCIAL ACTION ENHANCES THE LIVES OF ALL AMERICAN WORKERS. IN WARTIME AND PEACE, IN DEPRESSION AND RECOVERY, SHE ARTICULATED THE HOPES AND DREAMS OF WORKING PEOPLE AND WORKED UNTIRINGLY TO MAKE THOSE HOPES AND DREAMS A REALITY THROUGH THE FORCE OF HER MORAL COURAGE, INTELLECT, AND WILL. SHE BROUGHT SWEEPING CHANGES TO OUR NATIONAL LAWS AND PRACTICES AND FOREVER IMPROVED OUR SOCIETY.

SOURCES

Brooks, David. "How the First Woman in the U.S. Cabinet Found Her Vocation." *The Atlantic*, April 14, 2015. http://www.theatlantic.com/politics/archive/2015/04/frances-perkins/390003/.

Cohen, Adam. *Nothing to Fear: FDR's Inner Circle and the Hundred Days that Created Modern America.* New York: Penguin, 2009.

Colman, Penny. *A Woman Unafraid: The Achievements of Frances Perkins.* New York: Atheneum, 1993.

Downey, Kirstin. *The Woman Behind the New Deal: The Life of Frances Perkins, FDR's Secretary of Labor and His Moral Conscience.* New York: Doubleday, 2009.

Frances Perkins Center. http://francesperkinscenter.org.

"Frances Perkins." Social Security Administration. https://www.ssa.gov/history/fperkins.html.

Keller, Emily. *Frances Perkins: First Woman Cabinet Member.* Greensboro, NC: Morgan Reynolds, 2006.

Krull, Kathleen. *A Boy Named FDR: How Franklin D. Roosevelt Grew Up to Change America.* New York: Knopf, 2011.

Pasachoff, Naomi. *Frances Perkins: Champion of the New Deal.* New York: Oxford University Press, 1999.

Perkins, Frances. *The Roosevelt I Knew.* New York: Penguin, 1946.